# OUR WORLD IN COLOUR
# SINGAPORE

D1370192

# OUR WORLD IN COLOUR SINGAPORE

Photography by Ian Lloyd
Text by Ilsa Sharp

The Guidebook Company Limited

Title spread
*Sunset over the 'city-scape' of Singapore's central business district, Southeast Asia's Wall Street. This is the view from the southwest of Singapore island, at the Straits of Singapore that border the South China Sea. Just over 60,000 vessels use the port every year, making it one of the world's busiest harbours.*

Right
*The Singaporean typically reaches for the sky. Excellence, efficiency, service, quality, and cleanliness are among the virtues he values. The Republic's dynamic national airline, Singapore Airlines, epitomizes these virtues: here the airline's yellow-on-navy, blue bird-motif is carefully spruced up to match its image.*

Pages 6-7
*The port of Singapore never sleeps, clearing more than 500 shipping lines a year, 24 hours a day. Middleman to the world's trade with Southeast Asia, Singapore handles about 50 million freight tonnes of cargo a year, 32 million of them containerized, through ultra-modern facilities like this container terminal.*

Pages 8-9
*Recently Singapore has begun to refurbish architectural masterpieces like these. This 'Chinese neo-classical' architecture, so elegantly tailored to the tropical climate, is unique to Singapore and a few Malaysian towns. As a style it was at its peak in the early 20th century.*

Pages 10-11
*Highly disciplined when it comes to mass collective action, loyal Singaporeans line up perfectly in place at a National Day rally to form a human tableau depicting the red-and-white national flag, with its crescent moon and five stars. Singapore's National Day on 9 August is famed for such pageantry.*

Text and captions by Ilsa Sharp
Photography by Ian Lloyd
Edited by Nick Wallwork
Series Editor: Caroline Robertson
Designed by Joan Law Design & Photography
Production House: Twin Age Limited, Hong Kong

Printed in China

ISBN: 962-217-119-2

# INTRODUCTION

**I**NSTANT ASIA was once Singapore's own crude tag for itself. The implication was that the island republic, positioned at a world transportation cross roads, with neighbouring peninsular Malaysia to the north, eastern Malaysia (Borneo) to the east and Indonesia to the south, had almost all the attractions of the Southeast Asian region and that one need not travel further to find them. Certainly Singapore boasts a multi-ethnic blend of the region's peoples which is even more various than the bland official statistics of 76 percent Chinese, 15 percent Malay, 6.5 percent Indian and 2.4 percent 'Others'would suggest.

The mosques, temples, churches, synagogues and shrines of Singapore cater to an array of faiths, including Islam, Buddhism, Christianity, Hinduism, Sikhism, Judaism and Zoroastrianism. To appreciate the essence of this cultural jumble with its bright, shiny Western hi-tech exterior (visible from the moment you arrive in the dazzling chrome and super-efficiency of modern Changi Airport) and yet quintessentially Asian interior, you really need longer than the average visitor's 3.3-day stay.

This 636sq km (245.5 sq mile) island republic has passed through the industrial revolution to post-industrial society, all within the 30 years or so since independence in 1959 from the British. They themselves gained sovereignty over the island in 1824, five years after Sir Stamford Raffles had established a trading post there for the British East India Company, but this was certainly not Singapore's beginning. The island, strategically situated at the western entrance to the South China Sea, has been the linchpin in the ambitions of both the Indian and Chinese civilisations for centuries. According to Malay mythology, Singapore was founded by a prince. Having been washed ashore on the island he saw an animal he took to be a lion and, believing this to be auspicious, founded Singapura, the Lion City.

Singapore's political system is a British-style parliamentary democracy. The government is overwhelmingly dominated by the People's Action Party, which has been in power since 1959, led by Goh Chok Tong, recent successor to the towering figure of Prime Minister Lee Kuan Yew, architect of the nation. Never afraid of controversy, Lee was responsible for government-sponsored matchmaking for the country's well-educated in the belief that graduates breed graduates.

The result of this paternalistic government has been a highly disciplined, largely obedient people whose considerable natural energies are engaged more in the pursuit of wealth than in the arenas of politics, philosophy or the arts.

The PAP has signed an effective social contract with the majority of the people by keeping their rice bowls overflowing with the good things of life. Singapore is all that it boasts—safe, clean, and green. However, a new, better educated and affluent generation is now pushing for more of everything—for 'fun', more liberal arts policies, and more concern for heritage perservation—and often, they are getting it.

A determined push for industrialisation began in the late 1960s, partly as a result of the withdrawal from the Malaysian federation in 1965 and partly due to the economic shock waves resulting from the British troop withdrawal in 1968.

The combination of a natural national gift for commerce and a strategic geographic position at the hub of a booming region rapidly brought Singapore heady economic success. This success made possible enormous government housing programmes, to resettle Singaporeans from their traditional villages or *kampungs* into smart high-rise estates. These now accommodate 88 percent of the population. Yet this affluence and technological know-how have by no means completely erased remnant traditions.

The Singaporean Chinese businessman, sweeping out of his automated factory in a sleek limousine, might well be bound for a Taoist temple to consult the *fung shui* geomancer on where to build his new home. A suitably propitious location is as important to his success as economic efficiency.

The typically Straits Chinese blend of East and West can be seen in the windows and roofs of many gracious pre-war buildings. Straits Chinese (locally-born Chinese) trace their ancestry back to 15th-century Malacca in Malaysia.

Other buildings betray other strands in the tapestry that is Singapore — these slightly Arabic yet still colonial windows, for example.

Similarly, the Indian cashier at Komala Vilas, an old-favourite, vegetarian restaurant, still wears his traditional white *lungi* (wraparound skirt), hangs multi-limbed Hindu images and idols around his shop, yet he uses an electronic calculator to tot up your bill and his closed-circuit television helps him keep an eye on tables upstairs.

To add to the convenient confluence of Western comforts with the exotica of the East and the competing pulls of tradition and modernity are little gems of colonial history. The gracious nineteenth-century Raffles Hotel, a bastion of the British Empire, now lies in the shadow of the 73-storey Westin Hotel, that itself is part of a three-quarters-of-a-billion US dollar complex, yet this has not ruined the very special flavour of a Singapore Gin Sling sipped at sunset in the hotel's gracious gardens.

For the traveller, the chaos of cultural confusion that Singapore presents is a boon. It means Western comforts such as hot showers, bidets and US prime-rib, side by side with the exotica of the East.

Singapore is 'visitor-friendly'.Its people won independence from the British virtually without any blood being shed, they have kept the British street-names and lovingly maintained the nineteenth-century statue of their British founder Sir Stamford Raffles, set in the elegant colonial compound of Empress Place. Today the visitors are mostly tourists, but Singaporeans genuinely like foreigners, and they need to, for there are currently more than five million tourists swelling their own population of close to three million every year.

This phenomenon was gloomily foreseen by British snob J S M Rennie, who snorted in the 1930s: 'One is forced to opine that Singapore's main business will become that of a health resort and place of visit for American and Australian trippers.'

And so Singaporeans are kindly indulgent to the foreigner, rarely pointing out his blunders of etiquette. The visitor needs to learn from the row of shoes outside a Singaporean home that one should enter barefoot, and that the wet floor and bucket of water in a Singaporean bathroom indicate that most Singaporeans wash after relieving themselves.

There is no language problem for the visitor, however. The multi-lingual Singaporean usually speaks at a minimum his mother tongue, English, Malay, and often a couple more Chinese dialects too. Even his English can be spoken on two levels — formal and informal. The formal is for you, but keep your ears pricked to overhear Singaporeans talking informally to one another and you will find a kind of English almost incomprehensible to the outsider. It is a language that results from the combination of the dominant English language with Asian mother tongues. Jestingly referred to as 'Singlish' by locals, it is a vibrant street language, officially discouraged but flourishing nonetheless.

Once upon a time a pirates' lair and even not so long ago 'Sin City of the East' (as immortalized in Paul Theroux's '60s novel *Saint Jack*)Singapore has mellowed. The secret triad societies were rubbed out long ago and the last tiger—a circus escapee—was shot in 1902 under Raffles' billiards room so the legend goes.

Not that the glamour has gone. The new arrival still feels much as Joseph Conrad did in the 1880s, coming into Singapore harbour: 'I saw brown, bronze, yellow faces, the black eyes, the glitter, the colour of an Eastern crowd.' And you may still look from your hotel window, as Jim in Conrad's *Lord Jim* did, 'over the thickets of gardens, beyond the roof of the town, over the fronds of palms growing on the shore, at that roadstead which is the thoroughfare to the East—at the roadstead dotted by garlanded islets, lighted by festal sunshine, its ships like toys. . .'

This is still one of the busiest ports in the world, an international rendezvous for the very same adventurers and dreamers that people Conrad's stories, living 'in a crazy maze of plans, hopes, dangers, enterprises, ahead of civilization, in the dark places of the sea.' A global city.

This is a place too where southern-Indian Hindu Singaporeans, mostly Tamils, take to the streets every year between January and February with a cartwheel of spears piercing their body in the festival of Thaipusam, an awe-inspiring demonstration of piety for their gods.

It is also a place where you might turn a corner at the back of a skyscraper and walk straight into a classical Chinese street-opera. The makeshift stage is peopled with willowy maidens clad in Ming-Dynasty robes, and bearded warriors, their shoulders strangely adorned with waving flags, their faces grotesquely made up in black, white, blue and red. Together they wail in seeming harmony with the clash of cymbals and gongs.

*Sir Stamford Raffles, who first claimed Singapore as a trading post for the British East India Company, is revered by Singaporeans.*

If you relish the bizarre there is Haw Par Villa, with its grotesque grottoes and gruesome murals. Singapore has injected more than US$43 million to transform this one-time Chinese millionaire's playground into a 7.7-hectare pleasure park. The narrow back alleys of Chinatown are still here, although they have become safely sanitized hunting grounds for the shutter-bug. They still offer a fascinating store-house of oddities such as Chinese funeral goods. These are paper models of all the trappings of the affluent life from cars to televisions and computers, which are burnt at a person's death to ensure well-being in the afterlife.

The Singapore passion for food also endures. The old-style food-stalls still exist, but now in superbly clean new centres, both indoor and outdoor. Airconditioning makes the indoor restaurant more comfortable, no less 'authentic' than the outdoor one. Both still offer the same mouthwatering dishes — fragrant chicken-rice, oyster omelette, fried noodles, carrot-cake, Indian breads, Malay rojak salad and shashlik-like satay.

*The Merlion statue — a recently-created symbol for Singapore, the 'Lion City'.*

The favourite locations for this local 'hawker food' are Newton Circus, Cuppage Road Market, the Satay Club at the Esplanade, and a host of new food centres in prime Orchard Road complexes. Old stalwarts like the Rendezvous and Fatty's have moved into smarter premises but retain the style of old.

Seafood restaurants dishing out the famed chilli crab, garlic mussels (*tua tow*), steamed prawns and other shelled delights are often far from the sea nowadays—Palm Beach at the National Stadium, Long Beach at Bedok Road, Seafood Palace at pasir Panjang and myriad others—mostly along the East Coast.

New additions are classy but still good value for money, from upmarket Li Bai's nouvelle Cantonese cuisine at the Sheraton Towers Hotel, the charming chic of Prego's Italian restaurant in Raffles City and one of the best Western salad buffets in town at Pete's Place in the Hyatt Hotel.

New lifestyles have brought a few Western-style health-food corners like Steeple's Deli in the Tanglin Shopping Centre, but also a plethora of fast-food hamburger joints, swarming with young Singaporeans who seem mysteriously to prefer such imports to their own delicious fare. Fiery southern-Indian meat and fish curries are found around Racecourse Road in 'Little India', while the more spiritual, cooling qualities of first-class Indian vegetarian food, northern and southern, are served graciously in elegant surroundings by a religious cooperative at Annalakshmi (no alcohol and no cigarettes here), in the Excelsior Hotel arcade.

*The Supreme Court dome — legacy of colonial architecture of the 1930s.*

For those who can bear to give up the pleasures of the flesh, there are few meals more pleasing than a crisp Buddhist vegetarian one—at the Happy Realm in Pearl Centre, the Kwan Imm in Victoria Street, the Fut Sai Gai in Kitchener Road or the Loke Who Yuen in Tanjong Pagar.

The Hainanese-Chinese waiters of colonial renown still staff the elite Tanglin

*A Malay cultural dancer relives the vanished rural lifestyle of her forbears. Malays comprise 15 percent of Singapore's population.*

*Mother and baby watch the world go by — windows and doors are ever ajar in Singapore's humid heat.*

*Indians represent just over six percent of Singaporeans; most of them are dark-skinned Tamils of southern-Indian origin.*

Club and the Cricket Club as well as colonial hotels such as Raffles or the Goodwood Park (the latter with its Teutonic turret also claims nineteenth-century fame as the German Club).

Singapore has not only retained the traditional forms of its multi-cultural heritage but has also developed its own indigenous culture. The Straits Chinese provide perhaps the most developed example. They are Malayanized Chinese, who are descendants from the old Chinese families of sixteenth-century Malacca in neighbouring Malaysia, but who now are Chinese only in name. In Singapore the Straits Chinese have become distinctive for the Peranakan culture of the *babas* (male) and the *nonyas* (female).

There is an official preservation project at Peranakan Place and Emerald Hill Road, just off the Orchard Road tourist belt, dedicated to these urbane, sophisticated people, and also to their coconut milk and chilli-laced cuisine.

Recently Singapore has shown much greater respect for its own heritage. There are plans to preserve the old colonial area around the cricket pitch or Padang (as an area of museums and cultural centres), the 'Little India' of Serangoon Road, Chinatown itself, around the Singapore River, and Kampong Glam, which lies at the centre of Islamic Singapore.

The Kampong Glam is not always on standard tour itineraries, but is well worth a visit. In a humble alley called Sultan Gate (just up Beach Road from Raffles and past Arab Street) amid minareted mosques, Arab textile traders and Islamic calligraphers still cluster around the decaying palace of the one-time Sultan of Singapore, who leased his island to the British in 1819. Some of the residents in this area still use the Malay title of *Tengku* (Prince).

In the old colonial area the cricket pitch is flanked by the domed Supreme Court and City Hall. On these imposing steps in 1945 Lord Louis Mountbatten, British Supreme Allied Commander in Southeast Asia, took the surrender of the Japanese forces which had occupied Singapore in 1942. This did not, however, salvage British prestige in the eyes of Singaporeans who had seen their former masters humiliated by the Japanese.

The iconoclastic Japanese occupation together with the communist-inspired and racial riots of the turbulent 1950s and 1960s rank as the most formative historical experiences of the Singaporean nation.

Looming above the cricket pitch stands Fort Canning Hill. This was once the preserve of the Malay kings of the fourteenth century. Along Serangoon Road's 'Little India', pause to breathe in the aromatic perfumes of jasmine and spices, welter in the riotous colour of silk and brocade saris and the haunting drums and chanting of ornately decorated Indian temples, and have your fortune read by a brightly-coloured parrot that selects from cards on the pavement. Then head out of town.

Northward-bound along the Bukit Timah Expressway you will find Singapore's marvellous Zoological Gardens at Mandai, an 'open zoo' with no bars. On your right and left are the last remnants of the 130-million-year-old tropical rainforest that once covered all of Singapore.

The 75-hectare Bukit Timah Nature Reserve, which nestles in the centre of the island, complete with wild monkeys, flying lemurs, pythons, cobras and scorpions, is now a manageable forest, well-trailed and hard to get lost in. In 1855 man-eating tigers here almost provoked a serious emergency.

Towards the west is industrial Jurong, where the factories are skilfully camouflaged behind the greenery of the Chinese and Japanese Gardens. Here you can also see the Jurong Bird Park and its stunning, walk-in aviary, the largest in the world.

Island-hopping around Singapore's 57 offshore islands provides another escape route from the bustling city. Particularly attractive are undeveloped Pulau Ubin to the north and St Johns or Kusu to the south.

Sentosa Island, also off the south coast, sandwiched between Indonesia and mainland Singapore's Mount Faber, boasts a world-class wax museum, including a rivetting display on the trials of Japanese for war crimes held after the Second World War. Sentosa, which is underrated by jet-setting Singaporeans, also offers gentle country walks, specialized museums—the Coralarium, the Rare Stone Museum, the Maritime Museum, the Butterfly Park and soon an 'Underwater World' extravaganza—and some excellent, safe swimming off beautiful beaches.

If you go to the island on a weekend, the hordes of raucous youngsters shoulder-toting huge 'ghetto-blaster' cassette-players will remind you that Singapore is above all a young country. Like the young everywhere, it swaggers somewhat, but nevertheless has a vulnerable heart.

*More than 76 percent of Singaporeans are Chinese, most of them descendants of southern-Chinese immigrants. It is the Chinese who set the nation's cultural tone.*

Cool pastels and shady arcades distinguish one of Singapore's preservation projects, Peranakan Place, in Emerald Hill off Orchard Road. It is named after the locally-born and Malayanized Peranakans or Straits Chinese, masters of this style.

Old and new jostle for attention in Singapore's city centre. The 19th-century Cricket Club presides over the cricket green. The white clock-tower of the 1902 Victoria Memorial Hall is behind it, and the domed Supreme Court of the 1930s is to the right. Beyond Singapore River and the skyscrapers of the financial district to the southwest, lie the cloud-swathed hills of Indonesia.

An unusual side view from Bras Basah
Road of Raffles, one of the world's great
hotels, that dates back to 1887. Now
slated for restoration, Raffles was founded
by an Armenian family named Sarkies
and has become part of the folklore of the
British Empire.

Tall Travellers' Palms are synonymous with Raffles and its open-air Palm Court, where daily hundreds of Singapore Slings are served to admiring visitors. The famous gin sling cocktail was invented at Raffles' bar in 1915.

'Raffles stands for all the fables of the exotic East', remarked British novelist Somerset Maugham, a regular guest during the 1920s and 30s. Maugham wrote several of his stories at the hotel.

Constructed in 1887, Queen Victoria's Jubilee year, the National Museum building with its gleaming dome came to symbolize the museum's role as a centre of Western scholarship in the region. Today the building is also home to the National Museum Art Gallery with its permanent collection of more than 600 works.

The National Museum's rotunda lobby is covered by a soaring 90-foot-tall (27.4-metre) dome. A treasure-house of Southeast Asian artefacts (it includes a 3,000-piece jade collection), the museum is a fitting tribute to its namesake Sir Stamford Raffles, himself a man of science and an avid collector.

The Tan Kim Seng fountain sits in the National Museum grounds. In 1857 Tan donated S$13,000 to the colonial government of Singapore for the construction of a fresh water supply. The donation was disregarded by the authorities and only in 1882, prompted by a guilty conscience, did they erect this fountain in his memory.

The Singapore river has served as a major artery for trade and commerce. Old Chinese sampans and bumboats once wound their way along the river with the help of the eyes painted on their bows. Today the river is bordered by the gleaming skyscrapers of 20th-century Singapore.

Tropical nights are inviting after the hot noonday sun, and Singaporeans instinctively take to the streets for their evening meal, dining under the stars amid a festival of light and colour and a babel of sound. Street-side hawkers' stalls have traditionally offered the best, most authentic and cheapest food.

At the very centre of Singapore's premier shopping and tourist district lies the Orchard Road-Scotts Road junction. For decades, C.K. Tang's pagoda-style department store has been a landmark building for shoppers — the store, with its high-rise sister venture, Dynasty Hotel, still sits at this corner.

Singaporeans work hard, but they know how to play hard too. National Day, May Day and Chinese New Year are among the many festivals that give Singaporeans an excuse to get out on the streets in their fancy-dress best.

*The many smiling faces of Singapore: (clockwise) Chinese youth — in Singapore far from inscrutable; the Malay — ever gracious and sunny-tempered; the classical Indian beauty — colourful as a rainbow in her traditional sari.*

*The older generation still remembers a very different Singapore, whether under the British colonials up to 1959 or under the Japanese occupation from 1942-45, when Chinese resistance fighters waged a valiant guerrilla war with the invaders.*

Emerald Hill, painstakingly conserved, is a 'museum' of the elegant lifestyle of the Straits Chinese in the 1920s and 30s. The locally-born Straits Chinese were culturally fully Malayanized, and they were also social reformers and admirers of the West.

A Malay House, Singapore

As late as the 1920s, large tracts of Singapore were little more than swampland and tidal mangrove forest.

*Malay fishing villages built on stilts at the water's edge were still a common sight up to the mid-1960s.*

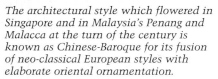

The architectural style which flowered in Singapore and in Malaysia's Penang and Malacca at the turn of the century is known as Chinese-Baroque for its fusion of neo-classical European styles with elaborate oriental ornamentation.

Typical of the style is the swinging saloon-door or pintu pagar entrance (top left) with its fine gold-leaf decoration, the ceramic wall-tiles on the lower half of the wall, and the barred, shuttered windows without glass for maximum circulation of air.

Old ways persist. The burning of joss or incense sticks keeps evil spirits away from the home. Here the housewife reveres the spirits of her ancestors in a prayer typical of local occultist-Taoist beliefs.

About 85 percent of Singaporeans now live in high-rise public housing estates provided by the government in a massive resettlement programme that began in the 1960s. Recently-built apartments are roomy and luxurious and most estates are now equipped with a wide range of amenities, including shops, schools, swimming pools and jogging tracks.

Approximately eight percent of Singapore's population is over 60 years old. True to Asian tradition, the government actively encourages family unity and rewards sons and daughters who keep their parents in comfort at home.

Coconut plantations in the northern and far western reaches of Singapore island, and on the many offshore islands, recall a rural past. More than half the island is built up now, and only six percent of it is farmed.

Fish farms abound in the more rural areas. With almost 40 fish farms, Singapore is a major exporter of aquarium fish, chiefly to Europe and the United States. The island exports more than S$47 million of aquarium fish and over S$4 million of aquatic plants a year.

Following page
The kelong, or traditional fish-trap, is a common and dramatic sight, silhouetted against the twilight skies of the seas off the northern coast of Singapore. At night lights are used to attract the fish into a huge fishing net which is suspended beneath the water in the area fenced off by the kelong poles.

*Childhood is particularly golden on a tropical island like Singapore, where youngsters can cavort almost naked in the sun and then cool off in sparkling waters. More than a third of Singaporeans are under 21 years old.*

*Village, or* kampung *life, especially typical among the Malays, persists in idyllic pockets like this. Malays who are also Muslims, live simple, traditional lives; they are very house-proud and also devout gardeners. Although they dislike dogs — as these are proscribed in the Koran — they love cats.*

Following page
*Traditional fishing boats*

Singapore boasts as many as 350 orchid farms. These gorgeous tropical flowers are native to Singapore and bloom in profusion here. With exports worth S$10.34 million annually, this is big business. Intensive research and careful breeding have produced many completely new hybrids.

Bamboo groves reminiscent of classical Chinese paintings are one of the glories of the parks and gardens in Singapore.

As the blazing sun declines in the late afternoon, the petals of the lotus unfold on the ponds and lakes of Singapore's gardens. The lotus symbolizes purity and is valued by the Chinese both as a medicine and as a food.

Jurong, on the western side of the island, prides itself on being more than a mere industrial estate. This Chinese garden, modelled on a 1,000-year-old Sung-Dynasty garden, is like an oasis among the factories.

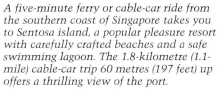

A five-minute ferry or cable-car ride from the southern coast of Singapore takes you to Sentosa island, a popular pleasure resort with carefully crafted beaches and a safe swimming lagoon. The 1.8-kilometre (1.1-mile) cable-car trip 60 metres (197 feet) up offers a thrilling view of the port.

Top right
A wax effigy of Lieutenant General Arthur Percival, the British army commander who surrendered Singapore to the Japanese in 1942 (in khaki, standing on the right), supervises the defeated Japanese as they in turn sign their surrender document in 1945. This is one of the many fascinating recreations of history to be seen at Sentosa's wax museum.

Bottom right
Sentosa's Musical Fountain: every night countless, luridly-lit water sprays leap and dance in rhythm to the tempo of lively music.

49

The call to the Muslim faithful echoes daily from the minarets of the gold-domed Sultan Mosque (1924) through the streets of old Kampong Glam, Singapore's Arab-Malay quarter. This quarter was once the royal preserve of the Sultan of Singapore.

Fort Canning Hill was once the Forbidden Hill of the Malay kings of Temasek, as ancient Singapore was then known. The remains of a British cemetery of the mid-19th century add to the aura of mysterious and at times ghostly peace that envelopes the graciously landscaped hill today.

The century-old streets and shophouses of Chinatown offer new surprises and delights at every corner, and not least of these is the architecture itself.

Singapore is the emporium of Southeast Asia and basketware fashioned from rattan, the springy, native cane, floods in from neighbouring countries to fill the island's bazaars.

In Chinatown garish Chinese calligraphy advertises merchants' wares and services from the shaded sidewalks. Older people live life much as they always have, bargaining over street-market fruit, or spending the hot afternoons away at the roadside watching passersby.

Chinatown, to the southwest of Singapore River, was set aside for the Chinese by Sir Stamford Raffles in his town plan of 1822.

*This mobile peddler hawks his painted masks, some funny, others grotesque or downright scary, from a wheeled card hitched to a bicycle. While some may depict traditional Chinese folk heroes, or opera roles, others represent Western cartoon characters such as Mickey Mouse.*

*A Peranakan or Straits Chinese wedding is a rare sight today. Here the nonya or Peranakan woman dons bridal finery for an elaborate ceremony traditionally lasting 12 days.*

Following page
*As local fruits come into season, Singaporeans take to the streets for an orgy of fruit-buying, pinching and sampling the goods shamelessly, haggling the prices ruthlessly. Among their favourites are the duku and langsat seen here.*

**Left**

*As well as finding tropical fruits native to Asia, you can get almost any kind of fruit from anywhere in the world at Singapore's fruit markets, including apples and oranges from the West, lychees and longans from China.*

**Above**

*You could write a whole book just about the prickly, stinking, sensuously-fleshed durian, the king of all Southeast Asian fruit. The durian is a Singaporean obsession, almost mystical in nature. Foreigners usually find the fruit and its odour a little harder to appreciate than local people do.*

**Bottom four**

*Singaporeans call these* kueh *(pronounced kway), using the Malay word for cake or biscuit. Kueh are nearly all brightly coloured, ranging from sticky red-for-prosperity Chinese ones filled with thick brown sugar or mashed sweet beans, to flaky sweet biscuits, to the truly Malay or Straits Chinese coconut slices and layered* agar-agar *(seaweed) jellies.*

Singapore's carnival is the annual Chingay Procession, a traditional Chinese celebration of spring, that is now usually staged the first weekend after Chinese New Year. A multi-racial synthesis of East and West, Chingay today incorporates everything from Chinese stilt-walkers and Malay and Indian horse-dancers (kuda kepang), to elements of Hollywood and Disneyland.

*Lunar New Year is the biggest festival in a crowded festive calendar and just about the only time the Chinese stop working. After a few days' peace and quiet during family reunions at home, the city erupts into a clashing of gongs and cymbals, a riot of lion and dragon dances, and the streets and squares are crammed with spectators and revellers.*

Thaipusam *is an awe-inspiring ritual. Devotees of the Hindu god Lord Subramaniam, son of Lord Siva, pierce their flesh with an elaborate cartwheel of interconnected spears and lances (the* kavadi) *in thanks for prayers answered.*

*Thus burdened, they sing and march the several miles from Perumal Temple in Serangoon Road to the Thandayuthapani Temple on Tank Road, home of the horse-drawn chariot of Lord Subramaniam. Very few of them show pain or even bleed. Singapore is one of the few places left in which to view this exotic ritual, for it has largely died out in its homeland, southern India.*

During the festival of Hari Raya Puasa at the end of the fasting month known as Ramadan, the mosques of Singapore are filled with the Muslim faithful. Muslims represent 16 percent of Singapore's 2.5 million total population.

Men and women worship separately. The men dress in wrap-around sarong-skirts and wear either the black songkok hat or the white skull cap, indicating that they have made the long pilgrimage to Mecca. This qualifies them for the title of Haji.

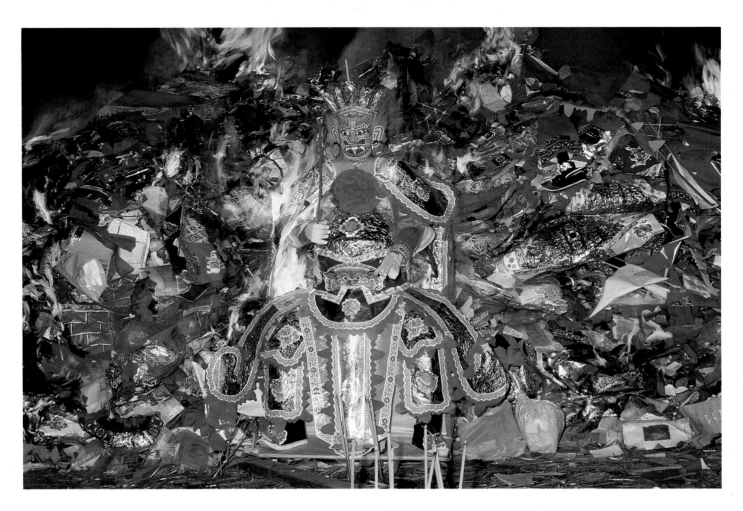

Doors, walls, ceilings and altars in Singapore's Chinese temples are richly adorned with a confusing pantheon of spirits, scholars, warriors, saints, gods and demons. This is typical of the multi-faceted nature of Buddhism.

Here the two traditional door gods guard the temple gates (left) and a paper effigy (above) of the Devil King goes up in flames at the Festival of the Hungry Ghosts. This falls on the Seventh Moon, when neglected and potentially evil ghosts wander freely in the human world.

Insect and animal symbols, as varied as butterflies and bats (the latter are believed to bring good luck), are important in Chinese religion and are frequently woven into temple hangings.

The dragon is one of the 12 creature symbols on the Chinese lunar calendar. In Chinese mythology, the dragon is a divine, auspicious and benevolent creature, in contrast to its role in Western legend. The year 1988 was the most recent Year of the Dragon.

Tiger Balm Gardens is the creation of the Aw brothers, more widely known as the manufacturers of the famous, cure-all Tiger Balm ointment, which made them millionaires. The Gardens feature scenes of morality and immorality, of Heaven and Hell; the effect is rather like a prolonged sermon in cartoons.

Few zoos in the world could offer you breakfast with an orang-utan, but Singapore's Zoological Gardens does. Here's a local star, the shaggy matron Ah Meng, with a Singaporean admirer. The Singapore zoo, set in 90 hectares of luxuriant natural jungle, boasts the world's largest social colony of the rare and endangered orang-utan ape from Sumatra and Borneo.

Colourful American macaw parrots greet the visitor to the Jurong Bird Park, another garden attraction nestled in the Jurong industrial estate. The 20-hectare bird park houses 3,500 birds of 400 species and the world's largest walk-in aviary.

*Chinese opera is as refined an art as Western opera or ballet. The stories are familiar to the audience, which understands the various stage conventions that compensate for the lack of reality and reads the actors' face-paint to identify the characters they portray. Here the black and white represents a villain and the pheasant-feathers a graceful female warrior. In Singapore, most operas are staged on temporary street stages and are known by the Malay word for theatre,* wayang.

Following page
*Singapore: glittering city of the future, a place where skyscrapers sit side by side with colonial monuments of the past, where the abacus shares pride of place with the electronic calculator and the computer, where East meets West . . .*

# An A to Z of Facts and Figures

## A

**Arab Street** Here beats the heart of Muslim Singapore. This is one of the oldest areas of the city and still surprisingly intact. Opposite the golden-domed Sultan Mosque, in North Bridge Road, are excellent Indian Muslim curry shops (the Zam Zam is the best known)—try a *prata* (flat-bread with curry gravy). But the real business of this area is textiles, carpets, basketware and all sorts of handicrafts from southern India and Indonesia. Great, cheap, enjoyable shopping and one of the last areas in Singapore where you can still hone your bargaining skills.

**Art and Antiques** Art has flowered in Singapore over the last decade or so, largely thanks to corporate patronage. Among the many notable names are Ng Eng Teng, potter and sculptor; Eng Tow, fabric and mixed-media abstracts; Thomas Yeo, oil and acrylic abstracts; Ong Kim Seng, nostalgic watercolours of Singaporeana; Goh Beng Kwan, striking mixed-media collages. Several galleries in Tanglin Shopping Centre stock their pictures.

If you're looking for antiques, the Tanglin Shopping Centre, Babazar Design Market in Cuppage Road and the little shops at the corner of River Valley Road and Clemenceau Avenue are all good minting grounds. Further out of town, antiques can be found in the Watten Rise district (Bukit Timah) a short walk from Coronation Plaza shopping centre, across the overpass from the Dunearn Road side.

## B

**Botanical Gardens** One of the world's great colonial tropical gardens, the 32-hectare Gardens at Napier and Cluny Roads are almost 130 years old. Here were nurtured the first Brazilian rubber-tree seeds which would found the huge Malayan rubber industry. The gardens have something for everyone: delightful little Victorian pergolas and bandstands, swans and lakes, impressive palm displays, a section of virgin jungle and 2,500 glorious orchids.

**Bugis Street** Enshrined in tourist folklore since the 1950s, this was once the favourite venue for sampling the sinful Orient in the shape of dirty pictures, sexy-to-lewd displays by flamboyant transvestites and various other dubious dealings, some of them centring around an execrable little public toilet, others in the opium dens off nearby alleys. It all went on long into the night. Having tried to close it down in 1985, the authorities have now had second thoughts, turned completely about and deliberately revived it, at a slightly different but nearby location, investing a cool US$6.8 million in the new-age Bugis Street—reopened in mid-1991. If you want to book a space in one of the shophouses overlooking the street, for your own private party, write to 6A Wan Lee Road, Singapore 2262, Tel: 65-2611367, Fax: 65-2610871.

## C

**Chinese New Year** You hardly get time to draw your breath after Christmas before the biggest non-Christian festival of the year is upon you, the Lunar New Year. It's the only time normally workaholic Singapore might just stop working, so don't try to do serious business at this time. The Singapore River is at the heart of the action with all kinds of special entertainments. The thing to eat in the restaurants is the special New Year dish, *yu sheng*, a raw fish salad with a lemony zing. Just before New Year's Eve itself (the night for families to sit down together at a reunion dinner), the Chinatown street markets are a wonderland of novelties, toys, gimmicks, food and fruit, as well as the Chinese equivalent of the Christmas Tree—pussy willow and mandarin orange trees, or chrysanthemums. At the end of the 15 days, it's time for the Chingay procession, which has mutated into Singapore's multi-racial version of a South American Carnival, featuring acrobats and dancers, dragons and lions and all kinds of processions and floats.

## D

**Deepavali** This Indian Festival of Light celebrates the victory of light over dark, good over evil. It's the best time to visit Indian temples and the marvellous shops of 'Little India' around Serangoon Road, which also has its own illuminations for this event.

**Dragon Boat Festival** Dragon-boat racing is rapidly gaining popularity outside of the Chinese communities in which it was born, and so Singapore's annual race, in mid-June, is attracting teams from all over the region, and the world beyond. The festival originates from the story that famous poet and statesman Qu Yuan drowned himself in protest against the political corruption and injustices of his time. Fishermen raced their boats out in an attempt to save him.

## E

**Empress Place Building** If you are a veteran visitor to Singapore, you may remember the mouldering old halls in the city centre where you formerly queued under whirring ceiling fans for the Immigration to renew your visas. In a Cinderella-like transformation, the 125 year-old Empress Place Building, has now been restored to its former glory at a cost of US$13 million and re-opened in 1989 as an elegant cultural centre-cum-museum, complete with restaurants and shops.

## F

**Fire-Walking** Known to the Tamil Indians of Singapore as *tbimi-thi* and usually held in October, the annual fire-walking ceremony presents a mind-boggling spectacle as devotee after devotee trots happily across red-hot embers. Get to the Sri Mariamman Temple in South Bridge Road early (the full rites begin at 2 am, but the fire-walking proper is in the afternoon), before it becomes a seething mass of humanity blocking your view.

**Fung Shui** Take a long hard look at your hotel when you next come to Singapore. It may not be quite as internationally standard as it looks. Is the cashier's desk strangely facing to the rear of the lobby, instead of facing the entrance doors like Reception does? Are the entrance doors set at an oblique angle instead of flat-on, or are they perhaps revolving doors? And is there a lot of water in front of the entrance—fountains and the like? If the answer is 'Yes' to all of these questions, it could be that you are looking at a careful exercise in the traditional Chinese science of geomancy, known to Chinese as *fung shui* or 'wind and water'.

It's a complicated science dealing with the best location and design for buildings (and graveyards), to ensure maximum happiness, harmony and prosperity. Dismiss it as mere superstition at your peril: it plays a big part in serious business decisions, like property investment. Oddly-placed doors may be designed to block out evil forces. Cash desks may be sited to prevent the money 'flowing out' of the front door. To face water is considered particularly beneficial.

# G

**Gambling** The authorities take a dim and restrictive view of this traditional Chinese addiction, but there are legal outlets such as the '40D' (Four-Digit, gambling on four-number combinations), the national lottery called the Singapore Sweep (S$2 a ticket, sold almost everywhere), and a traditional favourite, the horses at the Bukit Turf Club. There are races even when there are no horses in sight: the real thing rotates among the courses of Singapore, Penang and Ipoh (in the north of neighbour Ma-

laysia) on different weekends. Undaunted, the Singaporean punters still crowd the Singapore Turf Club on those 'away days' to watch the Malaysian races 'live' on an eighteen by six metre television screen. Contact Singapore Sightseeing Ltd on 7378778 for details of a half-day (six-hour) race tour package, including lunch.

# H

**Hari Raya Puasa** This Muslim festival is the high point of the year for Singapore's 15 per cent Malay population, and marks the end of the religious fasting month of Ramadan, fixed according to the Moon. During Ramadan, Muslims fast from sunrise to sunset, the more orthodox of them eschewing even liquids and the swallowing of their own saliva. For fasters and non-fasters alike, it's fun to visit Bussorah Street at this time. The street is alive with food-stalls and bustling housewives preparing to break their fast with wonderfully coloured cakes and all manner of exotic foodstuffs. At Hari Raya itself, the traditional Malay heartland of Geylang is also illuminated, its markets and bazaars extra busy. Everybody visits everybody else and you all eat fit to burst.

**Hungry Ghosts Festival** The Chinese equivalent of All-Souls' Day, the seventh lunar month is when the spirits of the dead roam the earth and visit their families. All sorts of rituals are necessary at this time to appease lost, resentful or impoverished spirits: mock 'hell money' is burned in roadside gutters, together with 'spirit passports'. Noisy street auctions are staged at which bidders offer far more than the value of what is being sold (food, altars, drink etc), in order to gain the gods' favour. Temples are especially worth a visit at this time and some exploration of back alleys may reveal a raucous street-opera or *wayang* in progress on a makeshift stage.

**Holland Village** A now not-so-secret shoppers' secret, this is still

the area to visit to get away from Orchard Road's thronging hordes. This genteel suburb lies just 15 minutes from Orchard Road, some way past the Botanical Gardens. With a long tradition of serving the British army personnel who were once based in Singapore, the shopkeepers in this area retail an astute mixture of local, regional and international merchandise. The handicraft, curio and antique-shopping prospects here are truly interesting and often cheap. There is also a fascinating mixture of eating-out options, both chic and simple, from British-style pubs and Mexican restaurants to good old Singaporean 'coffee-shops'.

# I

**Islands** Singapore's territory includes smaller islands to the north and south. Besides the well-known resort island of Sentosa to the south, there are also several other getaways worth the boat trip, some of them offering quite respectable coral-reef diving. Kusa (Turtle Island), a religious pilgrimage centre for both Buddhists and Muslims, St John's for its swimming lagoons and walking trails, Pulau Seking for its peaceful fishing villages, Pulau Hantu, a diving centre, and Sisters Islands for more relaxing beaches. Charter a 'bumboat' from Clifford Pier to get there.

# K

**Kucinta** An amalgam of the Malay word for cat—*kucing*, and for love—*cinta* (in both cases, pronounce the 'c' like 'ch'), this is the name picked by the Singapore Tourist Promotion Board for its mascot-cat the Singapura or Singapore River Cat ('Singapore's Love Cat' as the Board's poster has it). The Singapura, formerly ranked a mere mongrel alley-and-drain cat, has only recently been accepted by experts as a recognised breed, one of the world's smallest.

**Kiasu** A succinctly meaningful term in local dialect English which even Singapore themselves freely admit describes their national character. Roughly translated, it means 'Scared To Lose Out' or 'Must Win'.

## L

**Lee Kuan Yew** Although he has avoided the obvious trappings of a personality cult, Lee Kuan Yew's iron will and pragmatic philosophy have together influenced almost every aspect of life in Singapore since his People's Action Party (PAP) took power in newly independent Singapore at the 1959 elections. A Straits-born Chinese, his political genius was to perceive early the importance of the then active communist faction amongst underprivileged, Chinese-educated Singaporeans. He understood that his own people, the Straits Chinese, would prove too genteel and also too compromised by their traditional role as middlemen for the colonials when it came to the real crunch of the nationalist struggle. So he skilfully rode the communist tiger to power—and then promptly proceeded to tame it.

Singapore as we see it today is very much Lee's creation. He stepped down as Prime Minister only at the end of 1990, at the age of 67, and still serves in the Cabinet. His influence is still very much felt and his son, former Brigadier-General Lee Hsien Loong, is one of the country's two deputy prime ministers.
Several biographies exist, but none seems definitive—read the works by Alex Josey, TJS George or James Minchin.

## M

**MRT** Stands for Mass Rapid Transit, Singapore's mostly underground railway or 'tube'. Opened in 1987, it's a shining model of how it should be done. First, it's squeaky clean—no litter, no graffiti, not even any buskers, beggars or peddlers. Absolutely not any drug-addicts or pushers, either. Nor even the kind of pushers you get in Japan, to squash all the people into the trains. Stations and trains are air-conditioned, pleasantly bright and airy, feature original works of art and are super-safe. You couldn't commit suicide, or murder, on the tracks even if you wanted to, because they aren't accessible to passengers! Trains draw up behind a screen and align themselves with automated doors which then open straight into the train. On top of all this typically Singaporean efficiency, it's cheap.

**The Monkey and the Moon Festivals** The birthday of the Monkey God affords a rare spectacle at the Chinese Monkey God Temple in Seng Poh Road. The Monkey God's throne is paraded, accompanied by wildly prancing, entranced Chinese spirit-mediums who cut themselves and distribute paper charms to devotees.

Later in the year comes the Moon Festival known for colourful displays of Chinese lanterns (you can buy your very own at the shops in Chinatown or Holland Village) and the delicious round mooncakes, rich pastries stuffed with lotus seeds, red bean paste, nuts, salted duck-egg and so on. These sweetmeats were once used to foment revolution in old China, by means of secret messages stuffed inside the cakes.

## N

**National Day** Taken very seriously in Singapore as a major patriotic exercise, National Day is 9 August. Big bucks are often spent on lavish displays of cultural dancing, military tattoos and pyrotechnics. The usual venues for such spectacles are the National Stadium and the Padang—the old waterfront cricket pitch in the city centre. Or you can watch it relayed live on television.

## O

**Orchard Road** Orchard Road is where it's at, for the majority of tourists, serious Singaporean shoppers (and they really are serious), rubbernecking teenagers and all manner of good-timers. The action centres around the crossroads formed by Orchard Road with Scotts and Paterson Roads, marked most conspicuously by the pagoda-style skyscraper that is the Dynasty Hotel. This is fixed-price and sometimes pricey shopping territory. The road changes character with regular 'street parties' when it is closed to traffic. The huge gathering of Filipino maids around Lucky Plaza shopping centre on their day off, Sunday, is another of Orchard Road's curious phenomenon.

## P

**Phor Kark See** The full name for this, the most influential Buddhist temple complex in Singapore, is Kong Meng San Phor Kark See Temple. The first and fifteenth days of the lunar month are the times you will find it most alive, thronged with devotees and chanting monks, redolent with joss-stick perfumes. Tinkling bells and clanging gongs complete the picture. On these days you may sample the fine vegetarian cooking available in the temple kitchens—just make a donation. A sprawling complex of temples at Bright Hill Drive off Upper Thomson Road, Phor Kark See features some spectacularly sculpted marble statues of Buddhist deities such as the Goddess of Mercy, Kwan Ying.

**Population** Newly independent Singapore in 1959 inherited a population of one million, growing at an annual rate of four per cent. But the government's energetic family-planning programme was so successful that it brought the growth rate down to 1.2 per cent by the 1980s, with the population just heading for three million by the end of the decade. The planners have now reversed policy to encourage a three-to-four child family, supplemented by a selective immigration policy, fearful of a reduced labour supply, contracted domestic markets and the expansion of the old-people sector without enough young people to care for them.

## Q

**Qing Ming** Pronounced 'Ching Ming' this festival honours the ancestors of each Chinese family. Families dutifully troop out to the cemeteries to sweep and trim their loved ones' tombs, making offerings of fruit and paper money.

## R

**Raffles Hotel** Alas, poor Raffles, we knew her well... but she will never be the same again. Over 100 years old, the Grand Old Lady has emerged transfigured, at the end of 1991, from her chrysalis after a two-year closure for radical restoration and renovation at a cost of US$80 million. The goal has been to return her to the glories of her pre-Second World War incarnation. Rescued from a seedy 1950s rut, she will henceforth be very upmarket, and very expensive. A complex of bars, boutiques, gardens, a small theatre and a hotel museum attached to the main building will cater for both the well-heeled and the budget visitor alike.

## S

**Singapore River** The river was the original life-blood of commercial Singapore, a floating mass of boats and humanity plying in and out of the harbour. Old bridges dating back to the 1860s still span its waters and just as old are the *godowns* (warehouses) lining its banks, now joined by the glittering skyscrapers of the third richest country in Asia (after Japan and oil-rich Brunei). But the frantic to-ing and fro-ing on the river banks eventually led to pollution so serious

that fish could no longer live in the water. In 1977, the government tackled the problem in typically decisive style: they cleared all sources of pollution, including the traditional sampans. The big clean-up took them 10 years. Today, 30 different aquatic life-forms flourish in the river.

## T

**Thaipusam** One the great spectacles of the Hindu world, this festival can seem shocking to the faint of heart. A long procession of Tamil-Indian devotees streams between Sri Perumal temple in Serangoon Road and the Chettiar Temple in Tank Road, chanting and banging drums to help maintain trance-like states for those among them who carry the kavadi. This cartwheel-like structure of metal spokes is inserted through the flesh of the bearer, whose tongue and back is also pierced with tiny spears. Extraordinarily enough, no blood can be seen when these spears are inserted, nor when they are withdrawn—the reward of unquestioning faith, claim the devotees. They do it as a form of thanks for prayers which the gods have granted.

**Tanjong Pagar** This area on the periphery of Chinatown is something of a showcase for Singapore's new conservationist mood. Until only recently a sad and tired assemblage of about 200 old shophouses, it has now been refurbished, repainted and revitalised with an injection of traditional tea-houses, craft and souvenir shops, restaurants and pubs. Landmarking the area, at the corner of Neil Road and Tanjong Pagar Road, is the almost 90 year-old rickshaw station. Try lunch at the tasteful colonial-style Emmerson's Tiffin Rooms in Neil Road.

## V

**Vesak Day** Vesak is Buddha's birthday, an important festival on the Singapore calendar. In the Buddhist temples, caged birds are set free and saffron-robed monks chant through the day and night. Key locations to visit at this time are the Buddhist Lodge in River Valley Road, the Thai Buddhist Temple in Jalan Bukit Merah, and the Tibetan Buddha Sasana Temple in Jalan Toa Payoh.

## Y

**Yong Tau Foo** A kind of do-it-yourself soup dish commonly found at Singapore's food-stalls. You are given a pair of tongs and a bowl and you pick out the ingredients you want in your soup from a buffet display. Usually, there are various types of soy bean-curd, fishballs, stuffed chillis, bitter gourd vegetables and various leafy greens. You are expected to state whether you want a soup or a dry dish, whether you want fine vermicelli-type noodles or thick egg-noodles, and whether you want chilli. The stall-keeper then boils it all up for you.

## Z

**Zoo** Singapore Zoological Gardens, to be exact. Bordered by rainforest and commanding views over a huge reservoir lake, this skilfully landscaped 28-hectare zoo really is one of the world's most beautiful. It's designed as an 'open zoo', with natural barriers such as moats, or just the animals' own sense of psychological territory, replacing bars wherever possible. It features the world's largest social colony display of orang-utan apes and also tropical Southeast Asia's only polar bears, among a total of 170 species.

# INDEX

GS/08/02